CRACKING THE MARGIN CODE

Eight Steps For Wholesalers and Manufacturers
To Better Control Profits

CHRIS MACKEY

Published 2020

Million Dollar Author

Million Dollar Author Publishing
Sydney, Australia

Cracking the Margin Code. — 1st ed.

ISBN 978-0-6487202-8-7

Dedicated to everyone who has been told that you are slow at learning.

Written by a young boy who grew up in Griffith NSW, left school at 14 years and 7 months because his Dad said he was really not good at school.

It wasn't until later in life that I discovered that I was not "slow", I was just not diagnosed as dyslexic.

I find it impossible to read the way others do, and spelling is even more of a challenge.

We have other skills which more than compensate for dyslexia.

If you are like me and want to write a book, you will find the way to communicate your authority.

Only when the tide goes out do you discover who's been swimming naked.

— WARREN BUFFET

ABOUT THE AUTHOR

Wholesale and Retail Veteran & ActionCOACH Business Coach.

Chris Mackey is a wholesale and retail veteran with more than forty years experience in senior management roles for a variety of Australia's leading businesses.

His expertise includes National Marketing and Promotion Manager for a top 50 ASX company; General Manager of Campbell's Cash and Carry; launching the IGA Supermarket brand in Australia; and extensive international business operations training.

He now shares his wealth of knowledge to empower others to succeed in running their businesses. As an ActionCOACH business coach, he helps individuals recognize the value of their unique skills and to find creative solutions to their business challenges.

ACKNOWLEDGMENTS

When writing a book, there are so many people you wish to say “thank you” to.

To Brett Odgers my writing coach, Yvonne Lee, Caitriona Cohen and Cathy McBurney editors and proofreaders, thank you for your assistance.

CONTENTS

Dedicated to everyone who has been told that you are slow at learning. 3

ABOUT THE AUTHOR 4

ACKNOWLEDGMENTS 4

REALITY BITES 1

THE THREE PILLARS OF PROFIT 11

THE “5 WAYS FORMULA” AS A TOOL IN DATA STABILITY 16

DATA MASTERY 22

- A profit account 28
- A monthly profit and loss statement. 29
- A cash flow report. 30
- A break-even analysis. 30
- A debit and credit system. 31
- Profit margins. 32
- Key Performance Indicators (KPI’s) 33

THE BUSINESS PLAN 36

COST REDUCTION THROUGH NEGOTIATION 43

YOUR CRYSTAL BALL 53

KNOWING YOUR NICHE 61

CULTURE EATS STRATEGY FOR BREAKFAST 71

KEYS TO A WINNING TEAM 79

- Strong Leadership 82

Common Goals... 83
The Rules of the Game... 84
Have an Action Plan... 85
Support Risk Taking 86
100% Involvement and Inclusion of Your Team . 87
HOW TO GET MORE HELP IN YOUR BUSINESS
.... 93

CHAPTER ONE

REALITY BITES

In the past, when it came time to expand your wholesale / distribution or manufacturing business operation, you either borrowed capital to fund bigger premises or new locations. You had confidence that your business gross margin was significantly higher than your expenses. Therefore, you could take on more debt, without incurring a massive risk.

As a wholesaler, or manufacturer, you buy or manufacture stock and sell it for more than it costs you to produce it or buy it.

Traditionally, to expand, all you needed was the confidence that you could repay any capital from your healthy margin.

The reason that many of us went into business in the first place was to build a profitable enterprise. But somehow, over the last 15 to 20 years, the margins in many businesses have gone down. At the same time, costs continue to rise.

I remember being in a due- diligence team. The business that I worked in was acquiring a confectionary wholesaling business. I clearly remember the two brothers who owned this business, sitting at their office desk, opposite each other just looking into each other's eyes, not saying anything but clearly just on the brink of breaking down emotionally. They were just looking, not saying anything.

Hoping that one of the brothers was going to say to the other " Let's not sell our business. Let's not sell our dreams out". But the reality was that the guys knew that their business was not healthy. Its revenue was quite high, but the costs were increasing, and the margins were decreasing.

This business was these two owner's superannuation retirement funds. It was the nest egg they had worked so hard to build. Like many business owners, these brothers didn't draw a wage in the early days.

So, as I said, these two guys sat quietly, staring into each other's eyes, hoping someone was going break the silence and say, " Let's not do this".

The emotion was very real. There was no place for these guys to hide. They looked around the room and moved in their chairs and eventually the younger brother said, "Let's do this deal". They signed their contract and the deal was done.

Although it is easy to blame the coronavirus for the current state of affairs, I believe that the trend of lower profit margins actually started years before March 2020. This trend has led to many companies either having to close their doors or sell out on their dreams.

If you have survived, congratulations! You're lucky and you likely have the motivation to crack the margin code and get in control of this area of your business.

I was recently talking to a veteran wholesaler who had a family business for 45 years. I asked him what he thought was the biggest issue now, in 2020.

His response might surprise you. It was "people, people, people. See Chris, if you look after your family, if you look after your team, and if you look after your customers, everything else seems to always fall into place."

Cash Flow is also what your business needs. A business can be insolvent and still continue to trade if they have really good revenue. However, one day they will simply run out of the operating cash needed to pay their expenses.

Lastly, to grow your business without the risk of losing everything is ultimately what we need to be working towards.

One of the fears that businesses are facing, is that they are only dealing with the major corporations and this is putting more pressure on their margin.

I recently spoke to a manufacturer in Melbourne, Australia who, as a result of the coronavirus, had decided to only deal with major distributors.

He had stopped servicing independent business owners because he had a fear that they wouldn't pay their bills. This in turn was putting more pressure on his margin as the major distributors were buying at a significantly lower price.

There's also a hidden threat here if 80% of your margin is coming out of 20% of your customers.

That's a recipe for disaster.

If a buyer for one of those major distributors decides to change manufacturers this month, you could significantly lose business.

Here are three reasons why you should take some action today:

Get margins wrong and you're gone. A business with tiny margins struggles to ride any rough trading periods out. Success is dependent on the next big sale, which may or may not come. The business has no stability, you get the order, you fill the order.

There is a solid move away from buying products from China. Therefore, there are opportunities for you to interrupt the supply chains that traditionally existed and offer customers security around consistent supply and hopefully with your high margin products.

If you're not growing, you're dying. Business costs are consistently rising. When margins are not growing at a greater percentage than costs, your business is slowing running out of cash.

This reminds me of a tree that was planted on the outskirts of Sydney, Australia.

In the '60's my father would drive us to Sydney for holidays. We would pass a massive hundred-year-old fig tree that had been planted in a town called Picton. It had been planted by the owners of a large family-owned department store in Sydney called Gowings. On this tree there was a plaque that said, "If we're not growing, we're dying".

I clearly remember reading this phrase on that magnificent tree. I think it's also very relevant for your business.

The top generic skill in demand for the wholesaling and manufacturing industry right now is communication, according to this industry insight article:

https://nationalindustryinsights.aisc.net.au/industries/retail-and-wholesale

20 years ago, I'm sure that skill would have been sales. As our skills in the industry have changed, so

must the way that we look at our margin and cracking that margin code.

In this book, I promise you that I'm going to challenge you to think differently about the traditional way that you go about increasing your margin.

When I was a senior executive, working in Australia's largest food, grocery and liquor wholesaler, Metcash PTY LTD, I remember the CEO, Andrew Ritzer, every year would get all the executive teams together for an annual meeting.

One particular meeting was very profound for me because the CEO stood up and said, "I need you to go into your business units and break something".

I just sat there and thought that all the other people in the room must be so much smarter than me because I just didn't understand what he was saying.

What did he mean "break something"? Then the next thing he said was “If we don't break something, we run the risk of becoming ABDC - A Big, Dumb

Company". Aha, I thought, this guy really does know what he's talking about.

So, here's the challenge that I'm putting out to you:

Break your gross margin. Pull it apart and rethink it as we did in that Metcash meeting.

We had to go back and break something in our business so that we could put it back together, better than what we had originally and that's how we grew.

Crack that margin code and watch your business fly when you put it back together.

CHAPTER TWO

THE THREE PILLARS OF PROFIT

There are three pillars to growing your wholesale/ distribution and manufacturing business.

The foundation of any business is its data. Without data you are flying blind. Data gives you choices and having choices gives you balance in your life. For some, quality data can create a life you love.

Would your board a plane that is flying overseas knowing that the pilots had little or no data. The information fed back to a pilot on airspeed, elevation and the amount of fuel being used is not just important, but your life depends on it. Imagine the stress that a pilot would be under and how quickly they would burn out if they did not have this information.

When it comes to our business, we just hope we are okay. We starve our brains of the data that will give us the confidence to make choices.

This book is presented with three key take-aways.

1. Balance - have the life you love.
2. Freedom - developing a team that works so you don't have to.
3. Sell for profit - with certainty and forward momentum.

Balance will give you a life you love. Balance creates choices in your business operation. There are some key tools in your shopping cart for creating choices. They are:

- A plan to follow so you know how you are performing
- Mastery of your business foundations
- Key financial tools
- A dashboard that feeds you data and allows for informed choices.

When you don't have choices you really are at the mercy of your competition and your cash flow.

Freedom from having to do everything in a modern business comes from you learning new leadership skills and mastering how to get your team to follow you and eventually act on their own.

There is a famous quote, "Culture trumps strategy every time", and it's true. No fresh ideas or reaction to the marketplace will happen without a culture that supports new thinking.

I'm sure you've heard someone say that their business is not like it was when it started. They can't find or keep good people and if they want something done, they have to do it themselves. Maybe you've said those words.

We will delve into strategies you can use and why they are critical to getting you out of your to do list and setting up your business to run without you.

To sell your business for a massive profit is something most owners aspire to. Nothing in business ever stays the way it was. If you only "follow" on price, then you are only ever second best in the eyes of the marketplace. The reality, in many cases, is that price is not the number one reason your customers do business with you. 48% of customers do business with you because of the perception that you care about them and their business.

The potential purchaser of your business will pay a premium for a business that has the ability to adapt to changes in your marketplace.

When you build a business that can adapt to market changes; has a clearly defined niche; is not trying to beat the market leader on price only; is picking trends as or before they happen; and knows what not to do by learning from others' mistakes; then you will have a compelling business for buyers.

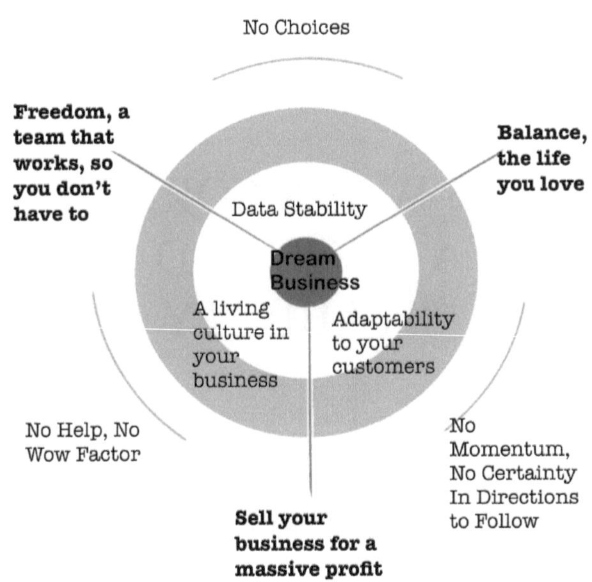

Picture yourself with your potential purchaser, a big smile as you say: "Come and let me show you how this business *WORKS*."

Pay day!

CHAPTER THREE

THE "5 WAYS FORMULA" AS A TOOL IN DATA STABILITY

If there is one universal language that bonds all countries and people together, then it is the language of numbers. Wherever you may be reading this book, numbers are the language of a business.

To understand what your business is saying to you, you have to learn to listen to what the numbers are saying.

Usually when I am invited into a business, the owner volunteers the information that the problem is not enough customers. To which I ask if they mean there are not enough leads coming in as a result of their marketing activities, or are they not converting all those leads into customers? Ten out of ten times, I get the same response, a blank face, followed by "what do you mean?"

Brad Sugars, the famous entrepreneur and founder of the global ActionCOACH franchise, in which I am a franchisee, discovered that customer revenue and profit are outcomes. Therefore, if we measured the activities that lead to these known areas of business, we can make changes and measure the changes as they happen, on a weekly and monthly basis.

Let's have a closer look at what Brad called the "5 Ways"

1. ***Leads*** - How many potential customers do you attract?

   X

2. ***Conversion rate*** **%** - How many leads do you convert into customers?
   = **Customers**

   X

3. ***The number of Transactions*** - How many times a year do your clients buy?

   X

4. ***Average $ Sale*** - How much do they spend each time they buy?
   = **Revenue**

   X

5. ***Margins*** **%** - The Margin your business achieves?
   = **Profit**

5 Ways to increase Profits

ActionCOACH

5 Ways to Increase Your Business Profits...

No. of Leads X Conversion Rate = No. of Customers X No. of Transactions X Average $$$ Sale = Revenue X Margins = Profits

Lead Generation | Conversion Rate | No. of Transactions | Average $$$ Sale | Profit Margins

Another way to think about the "5 Ways" is compounding interest. The multiplying effect is what gives business owners who work these numbers the massive effect they achieve.

Have you ever thought "why is it that my corporate competition just seems to be so much stronger than my business which is 80% reliant on price to have a great week?"

There are no secrets in business, there is only information you don't yet have.

Corporate business knows this and works their own version of the "5 Ways". Equally there are areas where you are performing really well. The point is that if you don't know what your average $ sale is, how do you know if it is growing from the activity you just did or is it just from luck?

A retail business I have worked with over the last six months has grown their average $ sale from $35.00 to over $45.00 consistently. To achieve this, we used scripts for the team and trained them on cross and up selling. There was a considerable amount of work on the mindset that you are not being a pushy salesperson, rather, when done with sincerity, you are actually helping someone to buy.

Could you imagine buying some beautiful cheese and getting home to find you have no crackers or buying some Gin and not being asked if you needed some tonic water?

Although the example above is a retail store, the same can apply to any wholesale / distribution and manufacturing business.

What is the best way to measure the leads you generate? Can it be enquiring via your web site? The thing is to have a number to measure that is actually what is happening, have a lead number. Although you may not be able to influence this number, you can make significant inroads into your conversion percentage.

As a thought, what does your business look like from a customer's point of view? How open and inviting is it? Have you considered a mystery shopper to give you some real information on what it was like to enquire about your delivery schedule or range?

There are endless strategies you can implement, your competition test and measure constantly. This is not saying that price is not important because, after all, you are in the most competitive industry there is. If everyone can compete on pricing, then how else do you grow? Knowing these 5 key numbers is a proven method and just by measuring your business activities your numbers will improve.

CHAPTER FOUR

DATA MASTERY

Have you ever noticed how some distributors or manufactures are so much more successful than others?

It's not a coincidence that the successful business owners seem to know all their numbers. You can ask them anything and the numbers are clear in their head, they can come up with the answer just like that. The majority of us though just get by with what's being deposited in the bank each week.

The language of a business is its numbers. They tell us everything that's happening within our business.

It's amazing that we have so many different languages in the world, but the language of business is common throughout all people of the world and that's why we can trade globally.

In this chapter, I'm going to focus on what we can do about our numbers in our businesses. Having a good working knowledge of data can be scary. A great number of us run away rather than learn what we need to know about reporting and what the business is saying. I totally get that.

Ultimately, we want to be able to read our data with confidence which leads to fantastic decision making. Decisions made with confidence get you closer to your goals, move you along a lot quicker than a decision based on gut instinct.

I believe the fears and frustrations that the majority of business owners have around numbers are based on what they tell themselves; “I’m no good at financial information” or “I just leave that stuff to the accountants, they tell me what is going on”, and that, in itself, is very sad.

You don't talk daily with your accountant, and actions you take today have an effect on tomorrow.

I think that we can do a lot to help people become very comfortable with what their numbers are saying about their businesses.

Business owners ultimately fear what the reporting in their business is saying. This thinking just builds frustration and frustration leads to procrastination and becomes overwhelming.

Now is the perfect time for your business to address the fears and challenges that data mastery presents. Otherwise these fears that have followed you through your life, just like in the diagram below, will keep repeating themselves.

There are three reasons why now is a great time:

Accounting software has never been cheaper and more accessible. Products like Xero are available on a monthly subscription, and even within those accounting software packages, there is entry level right up to ultra-professional. Therefore, there is little reason now for any business not to be running accounting software that will provide significant detailed reports.

Success and growth without data or without the right information is just not going to happen. It's critical, if not the gateway. If you want to grow a successful business, you're going to have to have accurate information on your business performance.

Peace of mind. We've never, in my memory, had so much stress and pressure put on us as business owners. A lot of that has to do with competition and a lot has to do with the fact that business has changed and is ever evolving and that's a great thing. However, imagine the peace of mind you would have if you had better control and a better understanding of the numbers within your business.

While holding a workshop a couple of years ago covering business projections, business planning software packages and budgets as part of business planning processes, I was shocked to learn how few business owners had no budgets in place and were not using any budgeting tools in their businesses.

These owners had previously worked for corporate businesses and had budgets that they were required to meet, and which were a mechanism of reporting to management on how their departments were performing; whether they were meeting targets and if not, what help did they need to achieve them.

Interestingly, they used the tools available because their remuneration was linked to the budgets they were given. When I questioned why they weren't implementing these tools in their own businesses now when it was their own and their families' financial security at stake, the response was astounding – nobody asked them to have a budget!!

Let's take a moment and think about what a budget is and why it's such a valuable tool. The purpose of a budget and the value you get from it is to tell you what's happening within your business now, historically and what next week and next month should look like.

Think of your budget as a little like driving your car. Should you drive it a bit faster (invest more into marketing or stock), or are you going a bit too fast (need more staff or a bigger selling area)?

It's a complicated topic, but one that shouldn't have you running scared. Consider it a management tool to let you know how you're performing against the goals that you've set. How is your revenue performing? Are you on track to achieve the revenue goal that you set? Are you making the gross profit that you need to cover the expenses that you have and, ultimately, are you making the profit that you deserve for the investment that you're making?

There are seven disciplines, which I'll detail below that I think are invaluable in any modern retail business.

A profit account

Traditionally, a business runs on its revenue versus expenses and what's left is the profit. I suggest that you open a profit account and start saving your profit. Pay yourself first, then pay your expenses. I've recommended this to many of the clients I coach and the difference that it has made is quite significant.

What this forces you to do is to only spend the money you should spend on expenses. I haven't come across too many businesses that are that disciplined, but imagine paying yourself first and why wouldn't you? You take all the risk after all, so you shouldn't only be paid what's left in the trading account at the end of the week. If there is no money in the trading account after you've taken your profit out, it's going to force you to look at your expenses.

However, you should be paid first. So, open a separate bank account. If, for example, you've budgeted to make 10%, which is 10 cents in every dollar, then move that 10 cents for every dollar of revenue every week into your profit account. I promise you that at the end of the year you will have achieved the profit that you wanted because you will have been forced to look at the parts of your expenses you overspend in.

A monthly profit and loss statement.

Set up an accountability session with your accountant, or if you're working with a business coach, make sure that's the agenda item for the first meeting of every month.

A profit and loss statement should be looked at weekly and monthly. After all, it's telling you whether you're making a profit or a loss. The purpose of this report is to give you the motivation to go and do something about your performance.

A cash flow report.

The most profitable businesses can fail due to cash flow.

Cash flow in any business is king. Having vision of potential periods where you will need access to your overdraft to cover expenses is key to peace of mind. To have a surprise that you have a short fall is not how to operate a successful business.

A break-even analysis.

Do you know at what point in any year you've paid for all your expenses? What about a break even for the month? What week of the month do you pay off your expenses and how about each day?

What time in the day do you break even?

If you knew those numbers and say that at three o'clock in the afternoon you had paid for all your expenses, but you were still open until nine o'clock, how would you feel about those additional trading hours?

A debit and credit system.

This is normally part of your accounting software package. The system is there to make sure you don't have any surprises and it's important that you look at it. It will enable you to forecast if you will be running out of cash in any week or month. Your accountant will be more than happy to offer you training on the accounting software of Xero and similar packages.

A reluctance to pay for the time is understandable, but in the long run accountants and coaches are there to help you on your journey. What is your peace of mind worth? Make the investment and go armed with questions and you will enjoy and learn from your time together.

Profit margins.

It sounds obvious that we know our profit margins, but do we? Do you know the profit margins of your departments? Do you know the profit margins of the key items within your departments? Fundamentally people sometimes get confused between mark-up and gross profit. If I ask “what is the gross profit of that department and get given a number which I know couldn’t be right, I realise the business owner is referring to the mark-up.

To explain, gross profit is the difference between what you sold the goods for, minus what you purchased the goods for at your cost, then divided into the selling price. A mark-up, as the word indicates, is the difference between your cost price and your sale price.

These two very different numbers are used for different reasons. I personally think that gross profits are more important than mark-ups because you pay your expenses out of gross profit. For example, you have a department with a gross profit of 40% and your expenses for that department are 45%, you can see there is a loss of 5%.

Key Performance Indicators (KPI's)

This is a reporting system that is very important and is missing from so many businesses. I'm referring to a KPI dashboard. A KPI dashboard is made up of five key indicators that the business owner can have at his fingertips that measure performance in the business.

Traditionally, you may have had your weekly sales as a key performance indicator. Instead, I would like you to measure something like the number of leads you generate. Measure something that you can change the outcome of. It's very difficult to change your sales as they are the result of the number of leads and the percentage of those leads you converted into sales. So, by measuring something which is an input, you can really have a lot of confidence in what's happening in your business.

The five key performance indicators can change the way you look at how your business is performing. Can you imagine not having to be so connected to your business but still being in charge and having confidence in what's going on. That's exactly what key performance indicators are designed to do.

You could be on holiday, you could be overseas or studying, and on a weekly basis, someone sends through what the KPIs are. It tells you that your business generated 5000 leads this week and converted 80% of those to customers. They are your first number and you know that everything is fine. Enough customers were generated this week and your average dollar sale was $35. You know exactly what's going on in your business without just being told what the sales are and what the revenue is.

I've been in business for over 40 years. Most of that time I spent as a Wholesale Executive. Reporting and the use of business intelligence was part and parcel of everything that we did and was a skill that we learned.

If you haven't come into the business world via the corporate route, then I understand the frustrations that you have, however it's like any muscle - the more you use it, the more comfortable you're going to get with it.

CHAPTER FIVE

THE BUSINESS PLAN

It's amazing how things that you experience in your past magically have an influence on your future. In 2003 I went on an executive leadership program provided by my then employer Metcash Trading. It was an intensive six months live-in course. We were asked to maintain our roles in the company as well as participate in this leadership program.

Little did I know at the time that one of our trainers was going to have such an influence on my life. His name is Major Terry O'Farrell, Australia's Special Forces. It was through meeting Major O'Farrell that I truly fell in love with the concept of planning, more specifically business planning. I got an appreciation from spending time with Major O'Farrell of how important planning is. Let's wind back the clock from 2020 to 2003. The training course was held in Wisemans Ferry on the outskirts of Sydney, in New South Wales, Australia. Major O'Farrell's role in the course was to help us as business leaders to understand the importance of planning.

Major O'Farrell took us through how the military would execute a plan for something as simple as crossing a bridge. To you and I that sounds quite straightforward but in a military context the planning that goes on behind the scenes to cross that bridge is outstanding.

Every conceivable situation is taken into account, not just where the snipers could be hiding to take shots at your troops but also when was the last time that the troops had a drink of water; where was their last meal; where is their ammunition; what's on the other side? It can be a six-month process that they go through for what seems like the simple process of crossing a bridge.

What really struck home to me though was when Major O'Farrell said "In business, if you put together a plan and something goes wrong, you may lose some money, you may lose some market share, but at the end of the day, nothing terribly dramatic happens. In a military context though, if the planning isn't meticulous a soldier doesn't come home."

That statement was so profound for me that I reference it regularly in my coaching practice when I'm encouraging my clients to really take into account contingencies.

That's exactly what the purpose of a business plan is. We can also look at the sporting arena for guidance in this topic. A sporting team doesn't take to the field without a game plan.

The team that has the best trained players (which is also part of the game plan); know how much training they undertake; where the training is held; by whom; whose job is it to score the goal; whose job is it to pass the ball. Every sport is meticulously planned, and numbers are used to measure performance. Those of you who are involved in sport at an elite level will relate to this.

If the military goes through so much planning for a simple thing like crossing a bridge and a sporting team meticulously plans everything from the nutrition of its players to the game plan, then I question how in business we just wing it?

We expect to open the doors and wait for the customers to arrive. We don't like to know how we are performing on our scorecard. Are you moving towards or away from your goals and dreams?

Consider your business is a plane and the cockpit is your business plan. A plane's cockpit is full of levers, gauges and switches and these instruments are all there to give the pilot feedback to keep the plane in the air.

Without this information the plane is likely going to fall out of the air and that is going to cost a lot of lives as in the military scenario discussed earlier. The instruments giving the pilot data on the action needing to be taken is what your business plan does to ensure your business stays on track.

Does every business need to have a business plan? The answer is a resounding yes!

When you're starting out there is no need for a 50-page manifesto, a simple one-page document is adequate, but you need to know how your business is going.

Are you on track to hit your goals even in the first month? If you've been in business for three or five years and you're fairly well established, a business plan is going to give you the tools to forecast and see what the future is going to look like based on your position right now.

If, for example, you have a five-year goal to own ten investment properties and you're at year three, and have three investment properties, you can be fairly assured that everything you're doing is working. However, a business plan will give you that vision into the future to decide if driving your marketing a little harder will enable two investment properties to be purchased in this particular year instead of just one, which puts you on another trajectory of creating more wealth and more generational wealth.

That's why I am a fan of a well thought out plan.

A business plan is not about having the meticulous attention to detail that the military has and then trying to apply that level of detail into our business environment.

I emphasise to all my clients and anyone who has succeeded in any business, that a business plan is possibly one of the best tools you can have. It gives you confidence to know that you're on track. It gives you confidence to understand what the possibilities are going to look like, what we must take into consideration, structure, strategy, positioning, and getting all these ideas down on paper and into a structure that is useable.

I don't want anyone to read this chapter and get put off or overwhelmed about what a business plan is. It can be as simple as a one-page document, or as elaborate as a 50 page, in depth plan.

It's all about what your plan is going to be used for. Are you raising capital for a new venture, needing to bring on an investor? Is your business well established and you'd like to consider the future and at what point in time you are going to optimise and sell? Your business plan can be tailored for all these things.

A well thought out plan is going to get you to your goals quicker than any other activity.

CHAPTER SIX

COST REDUCTION THROUGH NEGOTIATION

In this chapter you will learn how the top businesses around the world negotiate with their suppliers. As an added bonus, when you follow this process, you will be able to build stronger business relationships.

This chapter is based around my 40 years of experience in retailing and wholesaling, first as a buyer myself and then in leading teams and eventually divisions of buyers.

In it I will introduce you to a client that I worked with who reduced the cost of her inventory by 13% by following the teachings in this book.

Are you paying too much for your inventory or materials? Do you know how to negotiate effectively?

It's understandable that you only know what you know. However, in actual fact, you have been a negotiator all of your life. From the day you were born you've been negotiating with your parents, then family and friends. You went to school and negotiated with your teachers, got a job and...... I think you get the picture!

Wouldn't it be fantastic to be able improve these negotiating skills and put them to work? They will serve you in all aspects of your business, including dealing with employees, partners, suppliers, clients, etc.

Five years ago, I was running a training course for a group of account executives in Sydney who all thought that they were pretty hot-shot negotiators. Part of the course was about how to build stronger relationships with their buyers. I took them to the Flemington Fruit Market in Sydney and gave them all $25.00 and told them to go and create as much value as they could.

Negotiating with the vendors in the fruit market - pretty simple, right?

My hunch was that the tomato seller in the market was going to just eat them up and spit them out, which is exactly what happened. You see, he negotiates for a living. It's his whole life. His success depends on the margin he makes.

This is one of the things I am going to try to impress upon you in this chapter.

When I'm teaching negotiating to business owners in your industry, often their concerns are:

1. That suppliers will see them as just cash grabbers and that their reputation will be damaged, particularly in regional communities.

2. The growth of corporate giants in their industry is really starting to annoy them.

3. The reason they have never started to negotiate with their suppliers is that they don't know the process to use, or where to start.

4. They would like to take their business to the next level.

Do you share any of these concerns?

Building a robust process to get you some buying power is an integral part of creating more profit in your business. This will become more evident as you go through this chapter.

THE SYSTEM MODEL.

A FOUNDATION	B PROCESS
1. RESEARCH 2. LANGUAGE 3. LEADERSHIP	1. MAPPING ALL SUPPLIERS 2. KEY BUYER OF INFLUENCE 3. IDENTIFY NEGOTIATION PARTS 4. PREPARE INITIAL AGREEMENT ON NEW NEGOTIATION PARTS 5. NEGOTIATION PHASE (ROUNDS OF MEETINGS) 6. CLOSE THE DEAL 7. OPTIMISATION PHASE.

What I am going to teach you is not just academic theory. It is based on a real-life case study of a client who has a business in regional Australia.

It's also based on the fact that I was one of the top buyers within the grocery wholesaling industry in Australia.

So, I promise you, as long as you don't take shortcuts, everyone wins.

Negotiating is very similar to baking a loaf of bread. If you don't follow the recipe, or don't allow it to rise, you won't get the results you are looking for. The same is true for the instructions in this chapter - you can't take a shortcut. The steps I outline must be completed and they must be done in the sequence that I will guide you through.

This process works and it will work for you, as it has worked for the many others that I have taught it to.

As I mentioned before, I have a significant history as a buyer, first working for Coles Supermarkets for many years, then later on for Metcash, Australia's largest grocery wholesaler. I worked at Metcash for nearly 25 years and was ultimately responsible for leading divisions of buying teams across the whole of Australia.

During my time with Metcash, I attended numerous negotiating skills courses and have a certificate from the Mount Eliza Business School in Australia in negotiating.

Negotiation is a really great skill to have and it is something that you will never not use.

In the case study of A1 Hospitality PTY, LTD, (Not the real business name) I introduce the idea of negotiating with your suppliers for on-going rebate payments in the form of a fixed percentage of the money you spent with them from goods and services.

For example, if you purchase $100,000 in goods in a month, you get a 10% rebate. This means that the supplier will pay you $10,000 and, in many cases, you can deduct this discount from the total amount owing.

Let's get back to the case study. At the beginning of our coaching relationship, I suggested to Alice, my client, that she needed to negotiate for rebates. This blank shock horror came over her face. "Rebates Chris?" she said, "Rebates - aren't they just for the big players? That's something I don't want to get involved in".

Let me explain why we negotiate rebates and the reasons that they are your buying power.

Let's say that you are a supplier of lettuce for my wholesale operation. We negotiated and I successfully argued that I needed to save $10 on a box of lettuce. We both shook hands on this agreement.

Well, this agreement sounds good until you buy your next box of lettuce. Since it is fresh produce, there are lots of factors that influence costs, such as seasonal conditions, etc.

Therefore, if all you are asking for is dollars off, it is next to impossible to know what buying power you have. Equally, your supplier, over a period of time, can raise their prices to recoup that discount that they gave you. Trust me, it happens.

Another reason is that, unfortunately, there are no secrets. If your supplier did give you $10 off a box of lettuce, somehow, someway, one of your competitors will eventually find out. All of a sudden, your supplier has mud on his face, your competitor insists that they too need a better deal and the whole thing falls to pieces.

This is why rebates are the key to buying power. They are discounts off of your total monthly purchases that are either paid to you in the form of a cheque or as a reduction in what you owe for the account. This is why they are so much better than simply asking for a discount or better pricing. Rebates are ongoing and are not dependent upon fluctuations in the costs of goods.

So, the blood came back to my client's face once she realized that the secret was to negotiate for discounts rather than dollars off.

Negotiating for percentage discounts is the way to leverage your long-term growth.

Below is the step-by-step process to cost reduction through rebate negotiation.

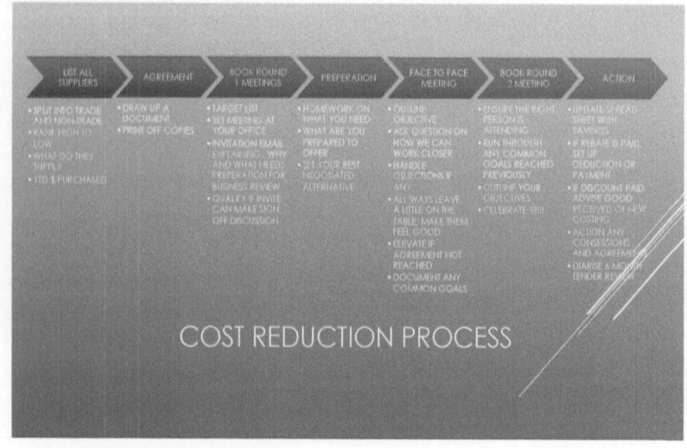

If you would like to go deeper and get a lot more details on the process and system, then my next book, "Buying Power: The Secret Art of Negotiating Deals" will be out early in 2021.

CHAPTER SEVEN

YOUR CRYSTAL BALL

Your crystal ball; the skill of picking the trend; what's in and what's out.

Some think it's a talent you're born with but it's actually a system and process. In this chapter, I'll show you a more scientific way and how to implement it in your thinking. How to be more informed with your decision making and connecting better with your customers to meet their needs and expectations will become clear.

Meeting the needs and expectations of your customers often before they even know how you can solve their problem is the skill of the marketer and the entrepreneur. We think we know what our customers want but often the facts tell a different story.

To have a wholesale /distribution or manufacturing business that is aligned with your community's needs, you must have new offerings that surprise and delight. Equally knowing what trend or fad is just about to start or is just about to finish is the true skill in inventory management.

Lots of businesses have the mindset that if you take a risk you may lose money, so they sit and wait for customers to ask for something. This is playing it safe. You're frustrated that your revenue is only slightly up on last year and there's no real growth. That all feeds into your fears of taking risks on new lines and new fads.

In my career in wholesaling and retailing, and when I was a buyer for Coles supermarkets and for Metcash trading in Australia, the key theme was that new lines or new offers are the lifeblood of the industry.

So, in 2020 and beyond, don't wait for a company rep to call before you make decisions about carrying a new line. The company rep has gone the way of the dinosaur and there will be fewer and fewer reps calling on your business, especially in regional and remote areas.

Even in the metropolitan areas you're more likely to see a merchandiser than someone who is trained in selling.

The decision on your range of products now rests with you, the wholesaler/ distributor and manufacturer. Remember that you can have anything you want in this life if you help your customers get what they want.

To rate as a marketer, I encourage you to get very familiar with your item movement reports and how to read them. If you don't have them already, create some to know where your stock is at any time and monitor it by setting up some trigger points. You can then be alerted when sales performance of the items that you're taking a calculated risk with start falling below your expectations.

Be aware of other markets and observe the trends and the tension that is being built.

During my career as a buyer in Metcash Trading, when a supplier came to my office to present new lines for consideration to be carried there were two standout qualities that I was looking for from the presentation.

I wanted to be excited by 50% theatre and 50% fact. Much of the decision making of a buyer for a wholesaler is based on how excited they get about the new product. If I got excited, the likelihood that my customer base would get excited and therefore purchase is high and reduces the risk.

You have to give your suppliers a degree of respect that they have spent energy, hours and significant money in investigating and bringing this product to market. They wouldn't be sitting with you if they hadn't already done their homework.

I'd also like you to have a documented process for how your business picks trends and decides on a range of products to have a significant focus on. It's a lot easier when you have this documented to be able to teach somebody else in your business how your company picks trends and new lines.

As mentioned previously, when to stop is as important as when to start. Picking trends and finding new lines is exciting and shouldn't be something that you shy away from. By doing this, if something isn't working out, you can view the flow chart of the process.

Understanding why this didn't work out will be visible in the process and you will clearly be able to say, this item or this trend failed at that particular point.

I mentioned before that I've had over 20 years' experience as a buyer for two of the major supermarket chains and during that time I also managed teams of buyers in the national corporate office and in all the states.

My teams looked after fresh food categories and all the different grocery categories including liquor. I was impressed a few years ago when I attended an Arnotts biscuit launch of new products for the upcoming winter season. As a company, Arnotts (which is the market leading biscuit manufacturer in Australia) has invested a significant amount of money in repackaging Tim Tams biscuits into bite size, bigger size and have come up with every conceivable flavour for their Tim Tams biscuits.

They're doing this to expand the market and to build on the success of the iconic Tim Tam biscuit brand as well as to find new markets to expand into. What struck me so significantly attending this presentation, was the sensory research that happens behind the scenes.

In my ignorance, I believed the new flavours were thought up by people in white lab coats coming up with new ideas and then testing these on the market to see how they perform.

I was surprised to learn how a new flavour or new product gets to market in a big company like Arnotts Biscuits. They can observe where and when trends start.

Let's think about the salted caramel flavour that's so popular. This trend started in food trucks and the local weekend market stalls. Then it started appearing in bakeries and cafes, so this was a second sensory marker. Until a company gets multiple sensory markers going off consistently, they take no action other that watching, it's like the ripple effect in a pond.

They don't react to the first ripple they see - it sometimes goes all the way to the fifth ripple before Arnotts is confident the trend they are watching is not just a flash in the pan. This trend or flavour profile is actually something that customers are interested in and therefore viable to go into a development phase to bring to mass market.

You can do the same in your business. If you are a wholesaler, look at what is on the reality cooking shows and notice where else you see something similar to the ripples in the pond.

If you're a liquor wholesaler, what is going on in cocktail bars and what grape varieties are being planted by growers that are experimental?

CHAPTER EIGHT

KNOWING YOUR NICHE

A business that has a defined niche just oozes confidence. They know who they really are and that's evident from the visual communication that customers are receiving about the business and the marketing messages undertaken.

A business with a defined niche knows who their business is there to serve. They don't waste money trying to attract people into their business who are not in the target market.

A business with a defined niche is also nimble in their reaction time to customers' needs and expectations. They're ahead of the curve and are flexible. I can promise you that in wholesaling and manufacturing, nothing ever stays the same.

Your ability to change tack, alter, and to find new markets is what is going to allow your business to grow, thrive and prosper with confidence.

If your business's mission is to serve everyone, in other words you're a generalist, then you are serving no one.

When we hear the word niche, we instantly think that means your business can only have one niche. This just isn't true.

A niche is actually about attracting and servicing a piece of the market better than anybody else. You are serving the customers that you love working with and they love the whole experience of doing business with your brand.

Let's step back and view your business through your customer's lens for a moment. Normally when we are thinking about niche and having a niche business, our minds run straight away to market retailing as an example.

Well, this could be true. Let's have a look at what Aldi has created. The niche is very clearly defined around cheap. There have been many retailers that have come and gone whose niche was also cheap, such as Franklin's Supermarkets and Jewel Food Stores in Australia. Knowing your niche makes your business run very smoothly, from the marketing right through to the cash register.

It's a seamless flow, not a chunky clunky flow, like a well-oiled machine. What a lot of business owners fear are is that by niching their business they will lose all other sales.

That is a scarcity mindset and there is no evidence that this happens. There is evidence that the opposite happens; that through niching, you can grow your sales because you are known for certain activity, range, and services.

Why bother developing a niche? There are things that your customers want most from you that you may be completely blind to. Therefore, the process of defining your niche may really open your eyes to what your customers want from you. It's also about the survival of the fittest. If you'd like to protect your turf, be the first into that market. If you can see an opportunity, so can somebody else and they will specialise.

This is why speciality food shops such as bakeries and fruit shops are positioned outside the major supermarket in a shopping mall. The fruit shop niche is that they have better quality and range than the supermarket. The reason, in the main, that they are successful is that enough of the supermarket shoppers are looking for that niche to make the business profitable.

The balance of shoppers who buy their fruit inside the major supermarket are doing so just about exclusively on the conviction that both businesses will be price matching each other.

Importantly, when it's time to cash out from your business, a defined niche will ensure that your business works without you.

I worked several years ago with an IGA supermarket in Victoria that wanted to have a vision of where the business would be in the next five years.

The business owner went through a significant and positive mindset change once we started looking into what his niche was. His mindset shifted from a broad range of grocery and perishable items to one more in line with what his community actually wanted to purchase. He undertook some structural changes and reduced his dry grocery range by 30%, made visual changes by re-painting and gave a larger footprint to fresh foods.

By doing these things he experienced a 10% revenue growth, and followed that up with 12% in year two, on top of the already 10% growth. The business was well on track to achieve another 10% revenue growth.

There is a significant amount of evidence that niching can deliver a better outcome than just being a generalist, the same outcomes will apply to your business.

To start the process of understanding what your niche is, or could be, you need to determine who you are currently attracting and why.

Does your business have a broad range of customers, with a dominant demographic you can detect, or is there perhaps a dominant age group?

Is there a clear average dollar spend that you can find? It's like trying to find a diamond in paper bags, and you will need to look under and around to identify who you're currently attracting and then understand why this is so.

The least amount of price competition happens with a well-defined niche because you add so much more value to the experience and that's what customers want.

They will pay for a great service and experience. If you remember back to my fruit shop example, consumers who want their fruit and vegetables to last at home for more than two days, will pay for this quality.

Once you've narrowed down who you are attracting and why, it's time to think about the market. An example is gluten free products, which are a trend right now and a dietary requirement for a lot of people.

The next step is to do a competition analysis. Is anybody doing what you plan to do within your marketplace? If so, do you still want to go down that path? If your answer is yes, you are now building some confidence that your hypothesis is accurate.

Additionally, don’t discount having a look in other areas where possibly you are not trading. There's nothing wrong with recycling somebody else's great ideas.

Next, identify your ABCD grade customers:

A Grade - your very best customers;

B Grade - customers that you are grooming to graduate to your A grade;

C Grade - customers that have the potential to be B grade, but equally can fall to D grade (investment in the C grade customers should be limited);

D Grade - those you should sack straight away. They don't value what you do. They complain all the time and cost you money to serve.

Work out some marketing strategies that talk to your A grade and B grade customers about your niche. These are clearly the people that you are meant to serve.

The last and most important aspect of this journey is to understand the investment you will need to make to enter this niche and what will you get for return on your investment.

If you're going to develop a niche in cheese for example, then that would require training, as the quickest way to not be successful is to think you don't need to learn before you earn. You might also need to buy some new refrigeration. Do you already have the talent in place, or do you need to recruit new team members?

To summarise, look at who you are attracting and why. Consider the market trend; is someone already doing what you are planning to do in your community or is it really an opportunity for you? Understand how to communicate to your A and B customers about your niche and less to your C and D customers. Look at your return on investment.

As the General Manager of a business called Campbells Cash and Carry Wholesale, I guided the business to 10% revenue growth and 101% net profit in three years by defining our niche into confectionery and snacks.

At the time there were a lot of small wholesalers and we could leverage our buying power to do a lot better job than they were.

Through our research and market analysis, we knew that the end consumer of convenience stores wanted snack food more than they wanted sunscreen and dish detergent from a petrol station or a convenience store. This is a clear example of how niching into the confectionary and snack food markets made a massive difference to a business in three years.

CHAPTER NINE

CULTURE EATS STRATEGY FOR BREAKFAST

Culture in a sporting team is the difference between winning and losing. A business culture is identical.

History will judge you on the legacy you leave the world, not the car you drive.

What you create is a culture that has lessons, not losses, and that never stops improving.

Committing to defining your business culture has financial returns as well.

No strategy that you try to implement will ever work without the support of your business culture. Can you imagine starting on a new sales strategy that your team doesn't support? You've lost before you even start. No-one should ever have to work in a toxic culture just so they can make ends meet.

I can certainly relate to having worked in a “boy’s club culture”, results at all costs. Have you ever heard a fellow businessperson say, “I can't get or keep good people”? In the majority of cases the person is in denial about the value of a culture, a defined culture.

Why does your competition never appear to have the same challenges as you? People are attracted to, not repelled by, a healthy culture. To quote Richard Branson, a businessman I admire greatly, “the first thing to look at when searching for a great employee is someone with a personality that fits with your company's culture”. Most skills can be learned, but it's difficult to train people on their personality. I think the obvious that Sir Richard is pointing out is his company had a defined culture from the very start, and then he set about looking for great employees. Is this person a good fit for our company culture? If so, I can teach them the technical aspect of their job.

There should also be an expectation that they have a level of competency in their skills. What will bring that employee undone is if they're not a great fit.

Where's all this leading, and how do you start creating the culture in your business?

What are the first steps? How do you go about documenting what your culture should be?

These are the four steps to take:

Write down the three values that are vital to you as the business owner.

As we go through and create your culture statement, those three values are not negotiable. We are going to get buy in from your team members, but just to stress the point, those first three values from you are not negotiable, so think hard.

I want you to ask your team to write down on a flip chart, the three values that are core to your customers buying from you again and again. Then ask them for the three values that are important to your team wanting to do their best. Next add the three values that are vital to your business success. That should give you 12 values and their words.

Take those words and look for the commonalities in the replies that your team gave because that's what they feel is the most valuable. Look for those common words and highlight them on your flip chart.
Now you need to create statements that support those values.

For example, my business has a defined 14 points of culture and number two is “ownership”. I am truly responsible for my actions and outcomes and own everything that takes place in my work and my life. I am accountable for my results–and I know that for things to change, first, I must change.

This is just a practical suggestion so you can create the statements that truly have meaning in your business, to your team and for your success.

There is a golden rule here. If you're going to create a culture, then we must agree not to have any motherhood statements in there. What I mean by motherhood statement is a statement that is full of words that have no real meaning, nothing of any substance such as "the biggest" or "number one". If the words can't be measured and are just there for filling out the document, then no one will buy into what you have created. It will be all for nothing. I can promise you this process will not work.

The next point I'd like to raise is how you can make this culture statement a living part of your business.

The creating of the statement is really just the beginning. How to change the culture in your business is the reason why you have made this effort.

The secret to making the culture a living part of your company going forward is to allocate one of those culture statements to everyone in your company.

Make them the champion for that part of your culture. What I mean by that is make someone the ownership champion within your company and on a regular basis, for example at team meeting, that person has to talk to everybody else in the company about how they have lived up to ownership. As part of the team meeting agenda, allocate a few minutes for that individual to talk about what ownership means to them personally.

Another of your cultural points might be abundance. Whoever you've allocated abundance to discusses what abundance mean for them personally in the business. I'd recommend that you rotate around everybody on a quarterly basis to ensure everyone takes ownership over a period of time of all the points in your culture.

As easy as it sounds, it really is important to ask yourself, who do you have to be? What mindset and commitment do you need to have to see this process through?

As Richard Branson pointed out, the culture was a massive part of the forming of his Virgin company.

It's the reason people did business with him; his culture was very, very different. Any of you who've experienced a Virgin flight can definitely remember how the staff, the flight attendants, the check-in team, everyone was a little different. Everyone who works at Virgin seemed a little happier.

I've worked with a number of businesses now on defining their culture. I recently had some feedback from a real estate business who I was engaged by to help with their internal and external communications. I put the whole team through creating the culture statement as part of the 13-week program undertaken. The majority of the employees all came back saying creating the culture statement was what they got the most out of from the course.

It's a very important part of a business and the difference between making it and faking it.

I encourage everybody reading this book to undertake this project as part of growing confidence in your business. It will repay you tenfold for the amount of effort that you put in and will make the difference between you and your competitors.

CHAPTER TEN

KEYS TO A WINNING TEAM

Have you ever wondered why some people in your team complete tasks with ease but still seem to be consistently working against you?

You care so much for your people. All that you're after is a fair day's work for a fair day's pay.

We think that everyone has or should have the same values that we do.

The reality is that no one has lived your life other than you. Your experiences and lessons are uniquely yours.

So, what is it that Wholesalers/Distributors and Manufacturers want?

They want to be able to find good people and be able to keep them when they do find them.

It's frustrating to have to do everything yourself in your own business and it's even more frustrating not knowing what you can do to get your team all pulling in the same direction, which is to serve your clients. Without help from your team, there is no "wow" in your business.

There's no way that you can, or should, be present in your business for the number of hours that it's open. Inefficiencies start to cost you money in wages when everyone on your team is not working together and harmoniously. When you are tied to your business your lifestyle and your family life suffers because when you're not there everything stops or stalls. That reason alone is why we need to learn new skills and the six keys to a winning team.

In Michael Gerber's book, “The E Myth”, a must read for anyone in business, Michael teaches why most small businesses don't work and what you should do about it.

His strong message is working **on** not **in** your business, a key part of which is working on yourself and therefore working on your business.

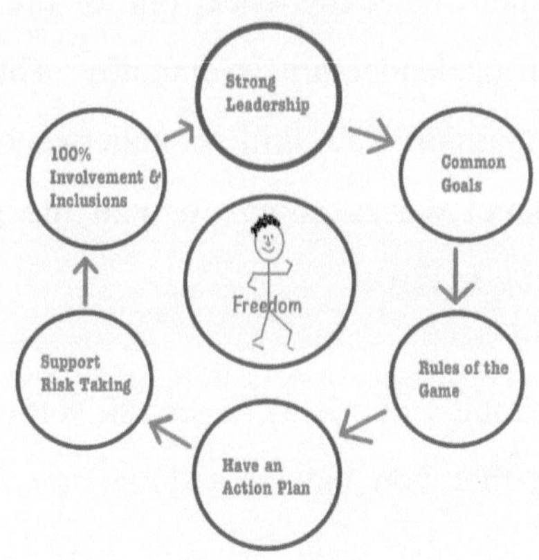

There are six key elements to a winning team:

Strong Leadership

The definition of leadership is the art of moving a group of people to act. Put even more simply, the leader is the inspiration for and direction of the action. They are the person in the group that possesses the combination of personality and leadership skills to make others want to follow their direction.

Let's take a moment and look at some of the skills a strong leader should have in a retail business.

From my personal experience, one of the key attributes of strong leadership is empathy. The ability to show compassion, the skill to understand at a very personal level what's going on with the person that you're trying to direct.

Another strong value is to never ask somebody to do something that you have not done or could not do yourself.

A simple way to look at that would be to lead by example. If you turn up for work dressed inappropriately, you can expect your team to do the same.

If you're not ready to work at the allocated time of your shift, why should your team, and if you don't speak to your customers and your team politely and respectfully, why would anybody else?

Common Goals

If you consider the sporting team again, everyone on the team knows what the goal is.

It's usually to get the ball or the player with the ball to the end of the field where he can score the goal. So, in a business context, it's very much the same.

What are we trying to achieve?
How are we going to achieve it?
How do we know when we have achieved it?

The Rules of the Game

Start with the end in mind when considering the rules of the game.

Have a recruitment procedure and system to follow. Building a great team starts with hiring them. Do they fit your culture, your values, your mission and the very fabric of your company?
Defining who your company is, and what the organisation stands for, gives the team the power to perform with the practical tools you have in your rules of the game.

Include detailed job descriptions, example duties, attributes, skills, knowledge, performance standards and some key indicators. These should all form part of your employment agreement.

People want to do a good job; they want to do the best job possible. If we don't set the guidelines and the boundaries for them to work within, it's no wonder we get the results we sometimes do.

So, start with the end in mind when recruiting and the framework for people to work within to achieve the best results.

Have an Action Plan

Start with understanding and auditing your team and ask your team to audit themselves.

You'll naturally find that they often score themselves harder than you would. From that audit you'll come up with an action plan. You'll clearly know where your team thinks that they need to improve, and you balance that with where you think they need improvement. Then create an action plan that's going to help them do their job better.

Employing a mindset that's all about helping your team do the best job they can is a lot more engaging than a business that is penalising in culture.

I'm sure we've all experienced working with someone, or maybe even ourselves, where the mindset is very negative.

Flip that around to a business that creates the coaching style of leadership, and we can then help our team do the best job they can.

Support Risk Taking

This is key to creating a winning team. Everyone understands the rules of the game, has an action plan, has feedback for areas of improvement and you are mentoring and helping them improve their sales.

Supporting risk taking can be very liberating for the business. This doesn't mean taking ridiculous and uncalculated risks, but if a team member has an idea that they want to try, support that idea. Have the individual work out some pros and cons, ask what is the worst that could happen if the idea fails or the best that could happen if the idea succeeds. Consider what lessons will be learnt.

Small Business in Australia has always been where great ideas are born and that's the reason business owners should have the confidence to support risk taking. Having confidence that the team are all working for the common goal is very liberating for you and it's certainly the catalyst to creating a 'wow' factor within your business.

100% Involvement and Inclusion of Your Team

This is the level where synergy is created! When one plus one does not equal two, but can equal 3, 4, 5, 6 or more. This can take the form of regular team meetings. You have to be disciplined to make sure these meetings take place. These meetings provide an opportunity for everyone to share their wins and focus on the positives, which creates a workplace where peoples' input is appreciated and actioned. We have all worked in a business that treats its employees as a necessary requirement but of little value to the business. That type of workplace is toxic and theft and sick leave usually run at high levels.

The owners just can't understand that as humans, we all want to belong to something.

The team should share what they're working on currently and what they need help with. Often, when working with a coaching client, I encourage them to have a 90-day action plan, based around the projects that they're working on. I encourage you to do this too. Make sure that this action plan is visible to everybody within the business. That way everyone knows the strategies that you're testing, the ideas that you're implementing, and what the intended outcome of those initiatives is.

This 90-day action plan can also form part of your team meetings, where you share with everybody the progress being made. I'm not advocating that you share information about your profitability but if you are trying a new strategy to increase your average dollar sales, then share it, and make sure everybody knows about it. That's what we mean by 100% inclusion - no surprises.

In my retail background, I worked for a large third generation family-owned company called Davids, which had outlets in every Australian state except Western Australia. The business culture of Davids was very insular which meant information was closely guarded within the family and a small circle of long-term employees.
This secrecy extended to the declining health of the business which suffered when the company tried to invest in areas in which it had no expertise.

I also worked for Metcash, the company that eventually acquired the Davids group. Metcash was a business which really did lead by example, from the CEO down. From the time the Metcash group acquired the Davids interests, everyone knew what had to be done. It was known that the business was in trouble and that it was up to the team to turn it around.

It was imperative to engage the suppliers and gain their overall support in order for the business to stay afloat. The strong leadership from the CEO and the board of directors meant that everyone knew the common goals, as dramatic as they were. A lot of the rules were made on the fly, but at least rules existed.

Later in my career at Metcash, I was the key person in launching the IGA supermarket brand in Australia, which was the epitome of a company supporting risk taking. They had a clear vision of what needed to be done and how the independent sector of Australia was being fragmented. Chain stores were continuing to grow because the marketing spend available was being diluted across 27 different banner groups, rather than invested into one banner group and getting every retailer to work together.

That's what I mean about supporting risk taking. There was a high probability that the strategy of launching the IGA group was not going to happen for months and months. It seemed impossible that we could get the retailers to agree to come together as one cohesive group under a banner called IGA, so even knowing the risks, the company went out on a limb to convince our retail customers to come together.

For my part, I had to raise all the funds to launch the group in Victoria and once successful, across Australia. I put together the marketing strategy to ensure that the end consumer also saw the benefit of shopping with this new banner group.

The other way that the business demonstrated 100% inclusion was through our renumeration. The company put everyone from the CEO, right down to the junior team, on a bonus system. The bonus system was all based on the same criteria. Obviously, some earned more than others but the matrix to calculate the bonus was all the same. One of the criteria was that the group had to grow, so not only did you have to grow within the group, but the first criteria was the total company had to grow before you were rewarded.

There were some very difficult times, but it was the first time in my life that I was involved in creating something which became a legacy. On reflection, I really see that without strong leadership, this never would have happened.

CHAPTER ELEVEN

HOW TO GET MORE HELP IN YOUR BUSINESS

We have an eight-step coaching program developed to guide wholesalers/ distributors and manufacturers in all areas of growing their margin.

Would you like to join us?

P.S. Whenever you're ready, here are 4 ways I can help you grow your business:

Connect with us on Facebook at

https://www.facebook.com/Mackeybizcoach

Or join our private Facebook group for up to date guidance and tactics on the five ways to grow your business

https://www.facebook.com/groupCrackingthemargincode

Or follow us on LinkedIn

https://www.linkedin.com/in/actioncoachchrismackey/

Or visit our website

https://chrismackey.actioncoach.com/

Or Call Chris Mackey: +61 437474556

www.ingramcontent.com/pod-product-compliance
Ingram Content Group UK Ltd.
Pitfield, Milton Keynes, MK11 3LW, UK
UKHW041844200726
13854UKWH00005BA/2049